# SPIDER MONKEYS

*by Vicky Franchino*

**Children's Press®**

An Imprint of Scholastic Inc.
New York   Toronto   London   Auckland   Sydney
Mexico City   New Delhi   Hong Kong
Danbury, Connecticut

Content Consultant
Dr. Stephen S. Ditchkoff
Professor of Wildlife Sciences
Auburn University
Auburn, Alabama

Photographs © 2014: Alamy Images: 5 top inset, 15 (Arco Images
GmbH), 28 (Bill Gozansky), 24, 25 (blickwinkel), 20, 21 (Christian
Musat), 32, 33 (Eric Gevaert), 4 background, 5 background, 8, 9
(Terry Whittaker); AP Images/Esteban Felix: 31; Bob Italiano: 44 map,
45 map; Dreamstime/David Lewis: 2 background, 3 background,
44 background, 45 background; Getty Images: 39 (Michael
Melford/National Geographic), 5 bottom inset, 40 (WILLIAM
WEST/AFP); Minden Pictures/Eric Baccega: 12, 13; Newscom/
Daniel Schreiber: 10; Shutterstock, Inc.: 36 (tamarasovilj), 1, 7, 46
(worldswildlifewonders); Superstock, Inc.: 34, 35 (age fotostock): 2,
23, 26, 27, cover, 16, 18, 19 (Minden Pictures).

Library of Congress Cataloging-in-Publication Data
Franchino, Vicky, author.
 Spider monkeys / by Vicky Franchino.
 pages cm. — (Nature's children)
 Summary: "This book details the life and habits of spider monkeys."—
Provided by publisher.
 Audience: 9–12.
 Audience: Grades 4 to 6.
 ISBN 978-0-531-21229-5 (lib. bdg.) — ISBN 978-0-531-25439-4
(pbk.)
 1. Spider monkeys— Juvenile literature. I. Title. II. Series: Nature's
children (New York, N.Y.)
 QL737.P915F73 2013
 599.8'58—dc23                              2013020242

Printed in China 62
SCHOLASTIC, CHILDREN'S PRESS, and associated logos are
trademarks and/or registered trademarks of Scholastic Inc.

1 2 3 4 5 6 7 8 9 10 R 23 22 21 20 19 18 17 16 15 14

FACT FILE

# Spider Monkeys

| | |
|---|---|
| **Class** | Mammalia |
| **Order** | Primates |
| **Family** | Atelidae |
| **Genus** | *Ateles* |
| **Species** | 7 species |
| **World distribution** | Mexico, Central America, and South America |
| **Habitat** | Tropical forests |
| **Distinctive physical characteristics** | Long limbs and long prehensile tail; the largest of New World monkeys; coarse fur and hairless face; lack opposable thumbs on their hands but have them on their feet; bodies are usually between 15 and 22 inches (38 and 56 centimeters) long; tails can reach up to 34 inches (86 cm); weigh between 13 and 24 pounds (6 and 11 kilograms) |
| **Habits** | Sleep at night and are active during the day; live in trees and travel by swinging from tree to tree; live in groups called troops; females leave the troop at puberty; males might stay with the same troop their entire lives |
| **Diet** | Omnivorous; mainly eat fruit; sometimes eat flowers, leaves, roots, bark, honey, bird eggs, insects, and larvae |

# Contents

# CHAPTER 1

# Life at the Top of the World

High above the jungle floor, all is quiet and still as a new day begins. Trees sway gently as a warm breeze sweeps through. Birds circle silently overhead. Suddenly, there is a rustle of leaves as a tree's branches dip and bend. A long arm covered in black fur swings into view. The day's peaceful start has been interrupted by the arrival of a spider monkey.

Thin and fast, this primate is well suited to its treetop home. Perched safely above many of its predators, the spider monkey stops to enjoy the fruit that grows throughout the jungle. It calls out to other members of its troop to come and enjoy the feast. The monkey swings from its tail. This leaves its hands free to gather food. After a hearty breakfast, it's time for the spider monkey to relax and enjoy the sunny day.

*A spider monkey uses its incredible tail and long limbs to swing through the trees in search of food.*

# Boy or Girl?

Spider monkeys are found in North, Central, and South America. They are the largest nonhuman primates found in this part of the world. Their bodies are usually between 15 and 22 inches (38 and 56 centimeters) long. Their tails can be even longer, reaching up to 34 inches (86 cm). An average spider monkey weighs between 13 and 24 pounds (6 and 11 kilograms).

It can be hard to tell male and female spider monkeys apart. They are very similar in height, weight, and features. The spider monkey's skin is covered in coarse fur. This fur grows in a range of colors, including black, gold, brown, and gray. The monkey's arms and legs are very long and skinny. It doesn't have hair on its face or hands, and its head is quite small.

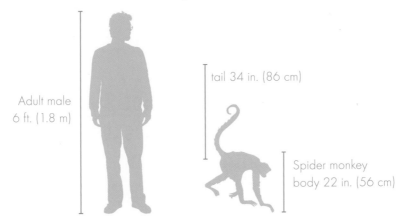

Adult male
6 ft. (1.8 m)

tail 34 in. (86 cm)

Spider monkey
body 22 in. (56 cm)

*Some spider monkeys have very light-colored fur, while others are very dark.*

# Treetop Home

Spider monkeys are arboreal. This means they spend most of their time high up in the trees. Spider monkeys' long limbs help them swing through the treetops quickly without falling. However, these limbs also make the monkeys very clumsy on the ground. Spider monkeys usually live in the highest parts of the trees. This area is called the canopy. It offers protection from many of the monkeys' ground-dwelling predators, such as pumas and jaguars.

A spider monkey has a number of tricks for dealing with dangerous predators or rivals that might steal its food. Sometimes it drops its waste from above. Other times it makes loud noises or shakes branches to make itself seem more threatening. If the monkey is very upset, it might even break off a branch and throw it down at the enemy.

FUN FACT! There are about 200 different kinds of monkeys found throughout the world.

*Spider monkeys are usually found high above the forest floor.*

# How Many Kinds?

Scientists organize spider monkey species in different ways. Some look at differences in fur color. Others consider where the monkeys live or compare their DNA.

Many scientists organize spider monkeys into seven species. The long-haired spider monkey lives in Brazil, Colombia, Ecuador, and Peru. The Geoffroy's spider monkey is found only in Costa Rica and Nicaragua. Some brown-headed spider monkeys have a brown head, while others are completely black! Black spider monkeys live up to their name with long, black hair. The Peruvian spider monkey looks almost exactly like the black spider monkey, but is slightly smaller. Brown spider monkeys have brown fur and live in parts of Venezuela and Colombia. The white-cheeked spider monkey has large, white whiskers.

*Black spider monkeys have darker fur than other spider monkey species.*

# CHAPTER 2

# Treetop Traveler

The spider monkey's body is designed for life in the trees. Its flexible shoulder joints make it easy for the monkey to swing from tree to tree. Its long arms and legs help it reach far ahead to catch the next branch.

Spider monkeys travel through the trees by brachiating. This means they move hand over hand. This is how kids use their arms when swinging on playground monkey bars.

A spider monkey's hands look like giant hooks. Most monkeys have opposable thumbs on their hands, but a spider monkey's thumbs are tiny. Scientists believe the thumb became shorter over time because it got in the way when swinging. Because of their tiny thumbs, spider monkeys are among the few kinds of monkeys that don't spend much time grooming their fur. The spider monkey does have opposable toes on its feet that it uses to grab on to branches.

*Spider monkeys can perform impressive acrobatic tricks as they swing from branch to branch.*

14

# Monkey See

Spider monkeys have very good vision. Their eyes face forward just like human eyes do. This allows them to judge distances very well. A spider monkey's good vision comes in handy as it swings through the trees and needs to tell how far away the next branch is.

Most male spider monkeys have dichromatic vision. This means they see all colors as blue, green, or some combination of the two. Most female spider monkeys have trichromatic vision. They can see all combinations of red, blue, and green. This doesn't mean the monkeys can see only three colors. It means they can see any combination of these three colors. Humans have trichromatic vision, too.

Scientists have found that it is common for diurnal animals to see in color. Diurnal animals sleep at night and are awake during the day. Being able to see colors helps them find food and travel safely in daylight.

*A spider monkey's forward-facing eyes give it excellent depth perception but keep it from seeing as wide of an area as animals with side-facing eyes can.*

# Smells and Sounds

Spider monkeys also rely on odors to learn about their surroundings, find food, and communicate. For instance, a male spider monkey has **glands** on its chest that create smelly liquids. It rubs these scents on the trees and the ground to tell rival monkey troops to stay away from its troop's **territory**. Female spider monkeys have their own special smells. These can tell male monkeys that they're ready to **mate** or can help baby monkeys find their mothers.

Spider monkeys use their sense of hearing to find fellow troop members in the jungle and to avoid trouble. But scientists believe their hearing isn't as good as a human's is. Their hearing is also not as good as that of many **nocturnal** species. If an animal hunts at night, it is often important for it to have good hearing because it is dark outside. Spider monkeys, however, spend their nights sleeping!

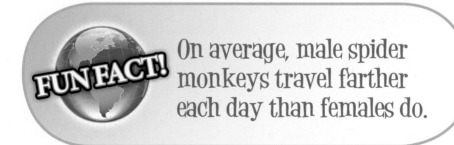

**FUN FACT!** On average, male spider monkeys travel farther each day than females do.

*As spider monkeys swing through the trees, their bodies rub against branches and leave scent trails.*

# Sweet Tooth

Spider monkeys have a good sense of taste. Their favorite flavors are the sweet tastes of fresh fruit. A spider monkey's diet can include the fruit of more than 150 kinds of plants.

Spider monkeys especially like ripe fruit. Fruit is very soft when it is ripe. A spider monkey doesn't have to chew the soft fruit. It swallows large chunks whole, along with seeds. As the monkey travels from one area to another in search of food, it leaves the seeds behind in its droppings. The droppings act as fertilizer and help the seeds grow into new plants. This is just one way that plants multiply and spread throughout spider monkeys' habitats.

A spider monkey will make do with other foods when it cannot find any fruit to eat. It sometimes eats other plant parts, such as flowers, bark, leaves, and roots. Honey, bird eggs, and insects round out the diet of a hungry spider monkey.

*Spider monkeys eat many of the same foods that humans do.*

# An Extra Hand

A spider monkey's tail is an amazing thing. This prehensile tail is strong enough to support the monkey's entire body weight. It is often longer than the rest of the monkey's entire body. A spider monkey can use its tail to hold on to tree branches and even to pick things up. When the monkey is ready to eat, it holds on to a branch with its tail and uses both hands to search for food. And when the monkey swings through the trees, its long tail acts like a fifth limb.

There is a bare patch with a ridged surface at the end of a spider monkey's tail. This is called a friction pad. This pad is similar to the tips of human fingers. It lets the monkey hold on to branches without slipping. No two monkeys have the same pattern of ridges on the friction pad. These patterns are unique, just like human fingerprints.

**FUN FACT!** No matter which species they are, all baby spider monkeys are born with pink faces.

*While all monkeys have tails, only some species have prehensile tails.*

# Something to Talk About

Spider monkeys communicate in many different ways. One is through sound. Spider monkeys can make a noise that sounds like the whinny of a horse. They can also bark, scream, squeal, whoop, and squeak. One sound might mean there is danger nearby. Another might let fellow troop members know that a monkey has found fruit to share.

Each monkey has its own unique voice. This lets other monkeys know whether they're hearing the call of a fellow troop member or a rival.

Spider monkeys also communicate through their facial expressions and body language. A spider monkey might shake its head or scratch its head or chest if it is upset. It could also arch its back or curl its tail. If a spider monkey crosses paths with a troop member, it might hug and sniff the other monkey as a greeting.

*Spider monkeys often show off their teeth to intimidate enemies.*

# CHAPTER 3

# Life in a Troop

Spider monkeys are very social animals. They often travel, sleep, and play in groups called troops. A troop typically has between 15 and 30 members. It can get bigger or smaller depending on whether there's enough food in the area and how many predators are nearby.

During the course of a day, the troop will split up and come back together at different times. The monkeys might split up into smaller groups when it's time to forage for food. Then they might come back together when it's time to sleep. The only other primate species to behave this way is the chimpanzee.

This structure helps spider monkeys in a number of ways. In a large group, they have more monkeys to choose from when picking a mating partner. It is also more difficult for predators to attack large groups. Splitting into smaller groups makes it easier for all troop members to find enough to eat.

*Troop members form close-knit bonds with one another.*

# Girl Power!

In most primate species, male monkeys leave their childhood troops when they become adults. Then they are in charge of their own troop. This is not usually the case for spider monkeys. When a female spider monkey reaches adulthood, she finds a new troop. Young males stay behind with their original troop. Female spider monkeys are usually responsible for planning where the troop will search for food. A female might also make decisions for her entire troop.

There is usually more than one male spider monkey in a troop. These males don't typically fight with other members of their troop. However, they are not friendly to males from other troops. If a rival monkey approaches, the troop will try to frighten him away by making noises and shaking branches. This can often intimidate the stranger and encourage him to run away. The troop will attack him if he still doesn't leave.

*Even though some spider monkeys are small, they can look scary when they need to.*

# Starting a Family

A female spider monkey is ready to be a mother when she is between four and five years old. She produces a special smell to tell males when it's time to mate. A female monkey can become pregnant any time of year.

A baby spider monkey grows inside the mother's body for seven to eight months after its parents mate. Most spider monkey mothers have one baby at a time. Their babies are born two to three years apart.

A spider monkey baby is tiny and helpless when it is born. It weighs less than 1 pound (454 grams). The new baby depends on its mother for food and protection. Its father does not help care for it. The mother **nurses** her baby and carries it with her. At first, the baby rides on her stomach. Later, it rides on her back. The baby spider monkey wraps its tail around its mother and holds on tight.

*Spider monkey mothers are very protective of their babies.*

# Growing Up

The strongest bond among spider monkeys is between mothers and their babies. A young spider monkey watches its mother and other older monkeys to learn how to search for food and protect itself. As it gets older, the young spider monkey will start to leave its mother's side for longer periods of time. Spider monkeys are fully independent when they're about three years old. In the wild, spider monkeys usually live to be about 20 years old.

Spider monkeys are very intelligent and learn quickly. Their brains are about twice as big as those of other monkeys that are similar in size. Their diet might be the reason for this. Spider monkeys eat a wide variety of fruits. They must be able to remember which are safe to eat and where to find them. Another reason might be the complicated relationships in spider monkey troops. The monkeys must form bonds with other monkeys and understand who's in charge.

*A young spider monkey travels on its mother's back because it is not fast enough to keep up with the rest of the troop.*

# CHAPTER 4

# The Monkey Family

Spider monkeys are part of the primate family. This family includes other monkeys. It also includes apes and humans.

Scientists divide monkeys into two major groups—Old World monkeys and New World monkeys. Old World monkeys live in Asia and Africa. New World monkeys live in North, Central, and South America. Scientists believe that New World monkeys traveled across the ocean from Africa to South America about 35 million years ago.

The two monkey groups are similar in many ways. They are all mammals. They have flexible fingers and toes. They usually have one baby at a time. Most species are awake during the day and sleep at night. Almost all monkeys are smart and very social. They all use their voices and faces to communicate.

*The black howler monkey, named for the remarkably loud sounds it makes, is just one of many New World monkey species.*

# Old World vs. New World

There are several ways to tell Old World and New World monkeys apart. Old World monkeys usually have small nostrils that are close together. New World monkeys have broad noses. Their nostrils are far apart. In most cases, Old World monkeys are bigger than New World monkeys and are more likely to spend time on the ground. Though they might occasionally eat insects or eggs, New World monkeys are more likely to rely on plants for their diet. Old World monkeys generally eat more meat.

Old World monkeys often have cheek pouches where they can store food to eat later. They also have opposable thumbs on their hands and built-in cushions on their bottoms. New World monkeys lack all of these features.

Old World monkeys don't hang from their tails. However, it is common for their New World cousins to depend on their strong, prehensile tails.

*The mandrill, an Old World monkey species, is known for its colorful face.*

# CHAPTER 5

# Disappearing Monkeys

The spider monkey is in critical danger. Unless steps are taken, this creature might disappear from the world very soon. All spider monkey species are considered vulnerable, endangered, or critically endangered. These terms mean that an animal is either at a high, very high, or extremely high risk of extinction in the wild.

Spider monkeys don't have many natural predators because they live so high in the trees. The biggest threat to their survival is humans.

When humans cut down trees to create farmland or build roads, spider monkeys lose their homes. They also lose their food supply and their way to travel from one place to another. Spider monkeys only like to live in primary forests. These are older forests with many large, mature trees. These forests have the fruit that spider monkeys need to live. Spider monkeys have nowhere to turn when their forests are cut down.

*Forest trees are often cut down to make wood and paper products that humans use.*

# Threats and Solutions

Spider monkeys are a source of food in some places. People who share the monkeys' forest home live in remote areas. They rely on any animals they can hunt to get enough to eat.

Global warming is another threat. Climate changes can affect the health of the forest and the monkeys' food supply.

What is being done to help the spider monkey? Some countries have created protected areas. No one is allowed to develop this land or hunt on it. Other countries have passed laws that make it illegal to hunt spider monkeys. For these laws to be successful, it is necessary to help the local people find other jobs and feed themselves. Ecotourism has been a solution in some areas.

Humans have put spider monkeys in danger of extinction. Now they must work together to find ways to protect these amazing animals.

*Wildlife experts are working hard to make sure that spider monkeys have a long and healthy future ahead of them.*

# Words to Know

**arboreal** (ar-BOHR-ee-uhl) — describing an animal that lives mainly in trees

**canopy** (KAN-uh-pee) — the upper level of a rain forest, consisting mostly of branches, vines, and leaves

**climate** (KLYE-mit) — the weather typical of a place over a long period of time

**dichromatic** (dye-kro-MA-tik) — a type of vision where an animal can see only in a combination of two color groups

**diurnal** (dye-URN-uhl) — describing an animal that is typically active during the day and asleep at night

**DNA** (DEE-EN-AY) — the molecule that carries genes, found inside the nucleus of cells

**ecotourism** (ee-koh-TUR-iz-uhm) — business that focuses on helping travelers learn about the environment

**endangered** (en-DAYN-jurd) – at risk of becoming extinct, usually because of human activity

**extinction** (ik-STINGK-shuhn) — complete disappearance of a species from a certain area or the entire world

**fertilizer** (FUR-tuh-lize-ur) — a substance that makes the soil richer so that plants grow better

**forage** (FOR-ij) — to go in search of food

**glands** (GLANDZ) — organs in the body that produce or release natural chemicals

**grooming** (GROO-ming) — brushing and cleaning an animal

**habitats** (HAB-uh-tats) — places where an animal or a plant is usually found

mate (MATE) — to join together to produce babies

nocturnal (nahk-TUR-nuhl) — an animal that is active at night

nurses (NUR-siz) — feeds a baby milk

opposable (uh-POHZ-uh-buhl) — capable of being placed against one or more of the other fingers or toes on the hand or foot

predators (PRED-uh-turz) — animals that live by hunting other animals for food

prehensile (pree-HEN-sile) — adapted for seizing or grasping, especially by wrapping around

primate (PRYE-mate) — a member of the group of mammals that includes monkeys, apes, and humans

species (SPEE-sheez) — one of the groups into which animals and plants of the same genus are divided; members of the same species can mate and have offspring

territory (TER-uh-tor-ee) — an area of land claimed by an animal

trichromatic (trye-kro-MA-tik) — a type of vision where an animal can see in a combination of three color groups

troop (TROOP) — a group of spider monkeys that live and travel together

# Habitat Map

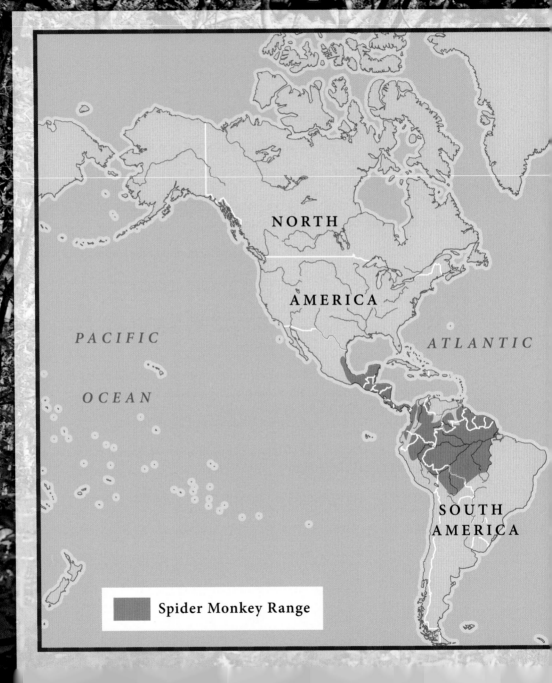

PACIFIC

OCEAN

NORTH

AMERICA

ATLANTIC

SOUTH
AMERICA

Spider Monkey Range

ARCTIC OCEAN

EUROPE

ASIA

AFRICA

PACIFIC OCEAN

INDIAN OCEAN

EAN

AUSTRALIA

# Find Out More

Books

Bodden, Valerie. *Monkeys*. Mankato, MN: Creative Education, 2010.

Gish, Melissa. *Monkeys*. Mankato, MN: Creative Education, 2010.

Schreiber, Anne. *Monkeys*. Washington, DC: National Geographic, 2013.

Visit this Scholastic Web site for more information on spider monkeys:
**www.factsfornow.scholastic.com**
Enter the keywords **Spider Monkeys**

# Index

Page numbers in *italics* indicate a photograph or map.

# About the Author

Vicky Franchino thinks it would be fun to swing from the trees like a monkey—especially with a nice strong tail for help! She is also a big fan of fruit but doubts that spider monkeys get to try out her favorite food: chocolate! Franchino has written dozens of books for children and enjoys learning about new kinds of animals. She lives in Madison, Wisconsin, with her husband and daughters.